tears for water

tears for water
songbook of
poems and lyrics

alicia keys

G. P. PUTNAM'S SONS ▪ NEW YORK

G. P. PUTNAM'S SONS

Publishers Since 1838

Penguin Group (USA) Inc., 375 Hudson Street, New York,
New York 10014, USA • Penguin Group (Canada), 10 Alcorn Avenue,
Toronto, Ontario, Canada M4V 3B2 (a division of Pearson Penguin Canada Inc.)
• Penguin Books Ltd, 80 Strand, London WC2R 0RL, England • Penguin Ireland,
25 St Stephen's Green, Dublin 2, Ireland (a division of Penguin Books Ltd) • Penguin
Group (Australia), 250 Camberwell Road, Camberwell, Victoria 3124, Australia
(a division of Pearson Australia Group Pty Ltd) • Penguin Books India Pvt
Ltd, 11 Community Centre, Panchsheel Park, New Delhi–110 017, India
• Penguin Group (NZ), Cnr Airborne and Rosedale Roads, Albany,
Auckland, New Zealand (a division of Pearson New Zealand Ltd)
• Penguin Books (South Africa) (Pty) Ltd, 24 Sturdee Avenue,
Rosebank, Johannesburg 2196, South Africa

Penguin Books Ltd, Registered Offices:
80 Strand, London WC2R 0RL, England

Library of Congress Cataloging-in-Publication Data

Keys, Alicia.
[Songs. Texts. Selections]
Tears for water : songbook of poems and lyrics / Alicia Keys.
p.   cm.
ISBN 0-399-15257-1
1. Popular music—Texts.   I. Title.
ML54.6.K48   2004   2004057325
782.42164′0268—dc22

Printed in the United States of America
3   5   7   9   10   8   6   4

This book is printed on acid-free paper. ∞

Book design by Stephanie Huntwork

To all my muses

poems

To all my muses

poems

from
songs in A minor

from
the diary of alicia keys

introduction

All my life, I've written these words with no thought or intention of sharing them. Not even with my closest confidants. These are my most delicate thoughts. The ones that I wrote down just so I could understand what in the world these things I was thinking meant. I would run to the bathroom, the smallest room in the apartment, but also the most private and personal, and there I would stay for hours, running the water to hide my tears, my fears, my confusion, my laughter, virtually anything that I was feeling, because I couldn't bear for anyone to know. I am private that way and I guess I always have been.

It wasn't until the process of going through all the words that I had documented in stacks of journals and notebooks that I realized how ready I am to share these "secret" thoughts. I have experienced all these things—some of them painful, some of them just observations, some silly, some that have affected me so deeply and with such frustration that the only way to express the confusion was to write it down. I want to share this now because I have learned from them, I have suffered through them, I have grown from them, and now I'm more aware of myself as a woman and as a person who goes through the things that cause life to be experienced in all its crazy, upside-down-sideways-inside-out-glory. I am more aware of what I feel and how to deal and where to go from here. Reading these words reminds me that all I've gone through and all I've seen wasn't in vain. It all adds up eventually.

I call this *Tears for Water* because in looking through all these words I have come to the understanding that everything I have *ever* written has stemmed from my tears of joy, of pain, of sorrow, of depression, and of question. Every single word has come from some form of my tears. I use them as water to nourish me, quenching the thirst for understanding myself, and because of them I am able to survive, I am able to stay alive, I am able to breathe. So I don't mind drinking my tears for water.

I know that any creative expression is destined to be subject to criticism, but this book is for me and all those who are on the search for freedom. For all who believe in the power of words and their potential to heal. These are for those of us who are open for anything.

I am opening my heart to you.

poems

golden child

Hello morning

now I see you

cause I am awake

What was once so sweet and secure

has turned out to be fake

Girl, you can't be scared

gotta stand up tall and let 'em see what shines in you

Push aside the part

lying in your heart

like the ocean is deep, dark and blue

Golden sunshine's

peeking through the grayness of the sky

Soon it will be in full view

and rain won't stain your eye

Girl, you be smart

look in your heart and see what shines in you

Push aside the part
lying in your heart
like the ocean is deep, dark and blue

You are a golden child.

You don't have to be afraid cause time is on your side
and they don't know the power you possess
or the beauty that's inside

Hello morning
now I see you
cause the lessons learned
these cards are the ones dealt to play
and the tables will be turned

You are a golden child.

I wrote "Golden Child" during one of the most devastating times in my life. It seemed like nothing could go right and everything I believed in was being tested and torn down. I felt like the most lonesome person on the planet. No one could understand my pain, nor could I explain it. It cut so deep I was almost numb. I didn't want to believe that was happening. I shut myself in a room with my piano and just sat there. Everywhere I looked, I felt out of place. The birds were chirping and the trees were beginning to bloom, but it was gray and brittle and cold. That's what people were. Gray and cold. They were monsters and I felt like I was slipping deeper into believing what they thought of me.

Maybe I know nothing.

I spent much of the day lying awake in a dark room.

own, unable to get up. I'm drowning. I have nothing and I don't know how I'm gonna get anything. Every time I go over that bridge I feel like a prisoner. I feel locked inside a world I can't afford. Things are getting tight. I gotta get outta here. But I'm numb. Everyone's numb. Nothing is right.

his was the turning point for me. I was forced to believe in myself and not in what others thought of me. It was one of the hardest lessons I've ever gone through, and it changed my life forever.

p.o.w.

I'm a prisoner
Of words unsaid
Just lonely feelings
Locked away in my head
I trap myself further
Every time I stay quiet
I should start to speak
But I stop and stay silent
And now I've made
My own hard bed
Inside a prison of words unsaid

I am a P.O.W.
Not a prisoner of war
A prisoner of words
Like a soldier
I'm a fighter

Yet only a puppet
Mostly I only say
What you wanna hear
Could you take it if I came clear?
Or would you rather see me
Stoned on a drug of complacency and compromise
M.I.A.
I guess that's what I am
Scraping this cold earth
For a piece of myself
For peace in myself

It'd be easier if you put me in jail
If you locked me away
I'd have someone to blame
But these bars of steel are of my making
They surround my mind
And have me shaking
My hands are cuffed behind my back
I'm a prisoner of the worst kind, in fact
A prisoner of compromise
A prisoner of compassion
A prisoner of kindness
A prisoner of expectation
A prisoner of my youth

Run too fast to be old
I've forgotten what I was told
Ain't I a sight to behold?

A prisoner of age dying to be young
To my head is my hand with a gun
And it's cold and it's hard
Cause there's nowhere to run
When you've caged yourself
By holding your tongue

I'm a prisoner
Of words unsaid
Just lonely feelings
Locked away in my head
It's like solitary confinement
Every time I stay quiet
I should start to speak
But I stop and stay silent
And now I've made
My own hard bed
Inside a prison of words unsaid

6:33 a.m.

Ask me what time it is?
6:33 a.m.
The way this looks
reminds me of someplace
I can only
almost remember.
That's why I think I feel so sad.
I remember it was always dark,
like this, outside
no matter what the time.
The bars on the windows
remind me of my loneliness
cause I would sit here
so all alone
on the black couch
and stare.
The shadows on the wall
make me lonely now
creating black and white rainbows.

6:33 a.m. is that time in the morning when all you feel is *everything lonely* and all you remember is *everything lonely* and you can't shake it. It was one of those dawns when you're startled by all your bad dreams and fears. I felt like I was back in a place I only knew in my childhood—a place where I tasted loneliness in every corner.

gold of johannesburg

I am changed
I know I am changed
Not for the worse
But changed indeed.

I am freed
I know I am freed
Not from the shackles
But from the lies

And since that is true
I know it is true
There is no prison
Except in my mind.

And songs of freedom
Are all that I own

Songs of freedom
Are all I'll ever have
And so I dream . . .

I am wiser
I know I am wiser
Not for the arrogance
But wiser indeed.

I have faith
I know I have faith
Or else evil ways
Would easily plant the seed,

But because my heart
Refuses to give up on love
And give in to fears
My strength holds strong
Through the bitterest tears

And so I am free
I know I am free
Maybe not of these shackles
But of these lies

And that's why
No matter how
Temptation tries
There is no prison
Except in my mind

And songs of freedom
Are all that I own
Songs of freedom
That can never be sold
And that is where I find
The gold of Johannesburg
The diamonds of Cape Town
The precious woods of the Amazon

And what I have found
Is all that has been taken from me
I have found
That I have been changed
I have been freed
But have not been tamed
And all I have
All I'll ever have
Is my worth and my freedom

They're not for sale
They have no price
For them I would give my life
It's all I'll ever own
And all I'll ever be
And so I stand.

lilly of the valley

Lilly of the Valley
Pale as the moon
Something in your eyes
Is tortured
Something is wrong
And it's hurting me.

Lilly
So soft and beautiful
So pure yet painted
By the evils of the world.

Lilly
Please don't let them
Crush your petals
And throw you to the wind

Lilly, please love yourself
From the roots deep within.

Lilly of the Valley
Don't dance for the evil one
Who cares nothing
For how precious you are
Or how tenderly you need to be picked.

Lilly
You are special
You are beautiful
And only should be treated gently
Like the breeze that blows
Like the spring sun.

Lilly
Please don't let them
Crush your petals
And throw them to the wind
Scattered
Leaving the residue of worthlessness on your lips
Forever lost
From what once was within.

1illy is a stripper. I am asking her not to let the world make her hate herself. I don't remember exactly when this came to me, but all my life I've seen women who've had to sell themselves in one way or another to make it. I've seen only the unexpressible pain in their eyes that it causes—leaving the residue of worthlessness on their tongues.

beckoning green

Beckoning green
come to me you whisper
roll in me, play in me
be free
you whisper
beckoning green of endless color
sage and forest the light reflects
come to me you whisper
Your flow is a dance in the wind
your voice is the spirit within
your smell is of the oldest fragrance
beckoning green
nothing matters when you're inside of me
you say
I am of your oldest dreams
your faintest memory
that place of lives long past

I will last

come to me you whisper

Play in my stems of long wheat

feel the ground and sand beneath your feet

take off your shoes and frolic in me

Beckoning green

beckoning me

get lost inside your dreams and visions

waving like the bluest ocean water would

but green

beckoning

Oh, Madrid!

What a sight you are.

this was how the landscape looked while I traveled to Madrid. I have a deep love for Spain but this was the first time I'd seen it at this daylight hour in the summer. Everything was so lush that I got this urge to break free from the moving bus and go to it. It was calling me and I had to listen. At the next stop I got off to find this deep, fertile land so I could touch it with my own two hands. I've never stood on land that green or played in grass as tall as me before, and felt so seduced. It was Beckoning Green.

damn you!

DAMN YOU!

For getting inside of me like this

For making me leave my cell

So I won't call

For making me feel so electric

By just one simple touch

Just the simple stroke

Of your finger on my neck.

DAMN YOU!

For wanting me so bad

That you make me want you

For trying to break down

My carefully constructed tough exterior

For trying to get close to the interior

DAMN YOU 3x!

· · ·

DAMN YOU!

For even making me write this down

For thinking this long about this

About you

DAMN YOU!

For making my never

Turn into a maybe

Turn into a never say never.

mind sex

Conversation

Stimulation

Good talk

Mind sex

Can you keep up or

Are you sleeping

On what

I've said?

It takes a whole lotta man

To understand

Good love is just

Stimulation

Conversation

Good talk.

So let's have sex

I wanna make love

I'd rather go to heaven
Can you take me above?
It's mind sex
Can we just talk
Can you make me feel it deep
Without a physical touch?

love in chains

It's bad to let the people you love go

because of your insecurities

yet it's so hard to resist

when you wish you could have more

Makes you wanna break free

I need stability

I know I'm stronger than this

but right now I feel so weak

There's got to be a better way to deal with my

feelings

Why did I have to fall in love?

I wonder

So instead I wrap my love in chains

Praying God will keep me from coming undone

Careful not to become too attached

to something I might, one day, need to let go of

Such a beautiful creature you are

so why am I so selfish?
Putting myself before you
knowing your love for me is mine to keep
Sometimes I feel as if I'm not sure
While you're on the phone
I listen with pain in my heart
am I right to stay and pray that it will stop?
Or should I leave before it hurts any more
As time goes on I stay and endure
and that feeling I get inside
your presence makes me realize
it doesn't really matter
cause I don't mind drinking tears for water
So I continue doing anything in the world
for you
Just to ignore that feeling deep inside
that I'm hiding
for me
Am I running from the truth?
When the fact of the matter is
things are as they are
and there ain't nothin' I can do
to change that
So I wrap my love in chains
Praying God will keep me from coming undone.

unfulfilled keys

There's a hole in my heart
When we are separated
I just want to touch you
Run my fingers up and down you
Feel you
But there's a hole in my heart now
Always so hectic
I feel as I've neglected you
But neglecting you is neglecting myself
And I miss you
Miss how together we played beautiful music
Of passion and soul
Of classic and heart
But now there's just a hole.

When I see one like you
It gives me joy

But just momentarily
For I can only pass and imagine that you were mine
Just a brief moment of imagination
And then I'm gone
I can't stay long
And so I feel all alone
And stupid
For maybe I have not tried hard enough.

Maybe in that dark moment
When all was so late and tired
I should have gotten up and come to you
I should've not made those excuses
And now
You're only to be found in fleeting moments
That don't really amount to much
And the hole in my heart gets wider and deeper
Threatening to explode
And outside I get more frustrated
And my fingers curl to a fist
Just looking for something to touch.

I miss you
I miss running my hands up and down
Your spine

I miss tickling you
And making you mine
I miss all of the time
We used to spend
With no interruption
And no need to end.

And now I'm yearning
With one hand on my heart
Shielding the hole
From the bitter wind
That will rip me apart
If I don't find your warmth soon . . .

I'm coming
I know you'll wait
Just don't leave me.

Unfulfilled Keys was a message to my piano keys and also a message to myself. I spoke of my piano as a man. Because that is the deep connection we have. But this is about my fear that I would never touch him again like I dream of. I felt like I had taken all our time together for granted. So my pain is real and deep. I remember writing it while walking. That was how powerfully I felt it. I couldn't even wait to sit down. I felt like if I didn't write it at that instant, everything would fall apart and my heart would start bleeding.

bus ride through
a periwinkle sky

Dawn creeping over the horizon

A lonely road far from home

The sun and the moon

Simultaneously risen

Shadows illuminated

Trusting in a higher power

As the man driving

Has my life in his hands

But the visions I see

Far surpass that morbid thought.

Sitting in a lone chair

All I've seen

It is a wonder

That I'm even there

Or here

Or anywhere
As I could be
This burning candle in front of me
Melting in a sigh
I could be a raindrop's cry
I could not be getting by
The sun is rising
In a periwinkle sky.
All roads lead home
But what's the direction?
Nothing is real
It is all just perception
Redemption
What does that really mean?
Better look it up so I can get in between
What a change needed
So long overdue
What are we going to do?
Really
I'm really starting to wonder now
I know what I believe in
But what if that's wrong now?
What if I'm wrong
Getting lost in the game

What if I just claim
To know myself
But we have yet to be introduced
Or reintroduced
It's like meeting a new person
Every day of my life.

There's a baby-pink ribbon
In a lavender sky
The shadows are turning into shapes of life
If life is a lie
Sometimes I wonder
Why I'm not being taken under
It's a prayer that awakens the inner dream
On which all is based
The race is internal
External's a façade of truth in a bod.

I don't know but I think I'm done
Rush hour traffic has begun
And here I am in this wondrous land
I never dreamed possible.

these thoughts came to me during a late night bus ride full of doubt, strength, and bewildered wonderment. I'm always up so late at night, so on the tour bus I like to sit in the two seats up front that look out onto the road before me. Watching the sky change color always makes me think about my most suppressed feelings.

the shore
(you sure?)

I'm trying to stay pleasant
But it's harder every day
I'm trying to keep my mind about me
But I feel like it's slipping away.

How can I give of myself
Yet to myself
Without confusing myself?
Am I a mess?
The city is beautiful
The experience is blessed
But at times I can't fix my mind to see it.

Wallowing in self-pity
Holding on for dear life

For deeper life
For my life
That no business deal cares for
So I must care for myself
Love myself
No one puts you down
And no one pulls you up
But where is the line?

Between self and selfless
Pleasure and pain
Life and death
Love and hate

Very dangerous lines
One or the other
A careful balance between
Sanity and none

Awash on the shore
Of love and determination
Alone with only your passion
Or will it be gone?
Lost somewhere in the sea

Of murky waters
Once so blue
      and
          clear
             and
                limitless.

constant evolution
of going nowhere

Here I am
Here we are
As it will go on forever
Noise, always noise
Candles burn
Lights are low
I haven't a place to go
Life in its constant state of moving nowhere.

The music is nice
Floats through the air
Sound of waves crashing
everywhere
Percussive submissions
Mind conditions
Righting with a left hand

Unknowing and taking the chance
Why not fly?
Why not try?
This constant game I play to
stay high
But all is just a state of mind
All is reality of your choice
Constant evolution
Constant adaptation
The constant state of moving nowhere.

Footsteps
Silence is loud
Kindness is brave
Wisdom is long
Loving is necessary
I need it
We need it
Searching
Looking for satisfaction
It is nowhere
It is everywhere
Pleading and praying
For God to come

What are we waiting for?
Why are we so afraid
Of taking charge

But it's always changing
Always
In the constant state of going nowhere.

We all have demons to battle
Roads to walk
Crosses to bear
Mistakes and sins
Candles and their steady glow
Water and its constant crash
Endless horizon
Rocks of times long gone
Still strong, still here
And so are we
Here we are
Forever
The constant state of going nowhere.

love with a shot
of distance

Does distance cause us to slip away?
Or is distance in the mind?
Is distance just the physical?
It can't be just the time away
That turns into change
It could be me so foolishly
Just caught up in a game
The game men and women play
But distance is so hard to bear
When it's happening so long
A breaking heart can't be justified
For the sake of a song.

Distance makes you slip
Makes you forget what you once thought
Makes you think you won't get caught

Gets you into what you ought

To know better

Yet it leads to the truth

If you take time to hear its whisper

Listen sister

To yourself

And don't slip away.

Love with a shot of distance

A potent drink

That can make you slip

Makes you forget what you once thought

Makes you think you won't get caught

Gets you into what you ought

To know better

That's love with a shot of distance.

The stakes are high

It's costly to try

When you're drunk you always lie

Just to get by

On love with a shot of distance.

cosmopolitan woman

I don't wanna be

No cosmopolitan woman

With big ol' city sophistication

And a façade of perfection

Every page of the story

Filled with predictability

Of a lost soul

A hole in your heart

Only filled up temporarily

By clothes

And money

And 101 ways to find Mr. Right

By sex and superficiality

Cause we've all lost sight.

⋅ ⋅ ⋅

No, I don't wanna be

A cosmopolitan woman

I just wanna be myself

I may not be perfect

But I am brave

May have pimples on my skin

But my glow is from within

I damn sho ain't cosmopolitan

And you won't find me on the cover.

Pages of a magazine rip and tear

With time the people are forgotten

Stories are outdated

But you'll never find a hole in my soul

And my story keeps growing

And only gets better

I have real skin that's tough like leather

I'm a go-getter

And I'm gonna win

Who gives a shit about cosmopolitan

Even only in my beginning stages

I'm more than just a silent woman

Frozen on white pages

Sick of these cages

But I am a lion

In my differences I am defiant
And that is more beautiful
Than any photo shoot
Than any cover story
Fixed with Photoshop
It's gotta stop
This image of beauty
Is all wrong
But it's been going on too long to realize
The prize is down inside the deepest region
Of your available soul
Behold
Read the story
And let it be told
Even in my beginning stages
I am more than just a silent woman
Frozen on white pages.

When I went to an AIDS clinic in Africa, I saw all these beautiful African women going through so much—they needed medication for their children and themselves to stay alive. The only magazines that I saw in the clinic were magazines like *Cosmopolitan*, with white models' faces on the covers, looking healthy and unaware of the world these women live in. At that moment it wasn't about race or color; it was about what some magazines represent. And I felt horrified that they were the only things on the tables to be read. So I wrote.

still water

Still Water won't never come clean
No place to run from himself.
From afar Still Water looks magical,
Peaceful, strong, dark and deep.
It's not till you come close
That you see his murky waters
How shallow he really is
The deep darkness isn't only what's clouding his
    clearness.
Still Water won't never come clean
He's dirty and mean
Polluted by his environment
Ain't never been treated good.
Even the cute ducks shit in his waters
Leaving feathers and debris
There's no way he'll ever run free.
Stuck in a hole

Made by man to keep him contained, constrained,

Trapped, disgustingly disgusted and disguised

Getting dirtier by the minute.

Still Water won't never come clean

Cause now he's too conditioned to move

And even if the drain opened

and all the dark dirty waters could freely run

Into the strong-moving ever-changing ocean

He wouldn't go

Cause Still Water won't never come clean

Cause Still Water's whole soul is polluted.

Even the beautiful bird that sees him from afar

And wants to experience what she sees as beauty

Can't survive

He only drowns her in mud and self-pity

It's a never-winning game of love.

Every wonder why dirty ducks flock to a dingy pond?

They are all he deserves

They are the mirror of Still Water's heart.

is it insane?

Is it insane?
My life's in your love's hands
Is it insane?
How you've got a hold on me.

When you're near
all of me trembles
slightest touch
and I'm no good
and when you walk out of my door
I want you more.

Is it insane?
I was the one who called them fools
for being blinded by love

now it's me
who can't break free.

Even though you're with her
I still feel you in me
and I know when you kiss her
you're wishing that it was me.

Is it insane?
Thought you'd be my king
I'd be your queen
it would be complete with a wedding ring
was that just me imagining?

Now I cry
like I'm your widow
without you
I can't contain
this is my soul's last refrain
and you're the one that I blame.

She can have you now
I just want to fade away
sacrifice my life

to relieve this pain
so much pain.

Lord! Take away the pain!!

Is it insane?

in my search
for heaven

Is it a game we play

Every day of our lives

trying to find

what we believe

trying to learn what is right?

So many mistakes I've made

so many times

so many tears

Trying to learn to live

with these regrets of mine

Still it makes me feel like shit

feels like damn

feels like I'm burning inside

It makes me feel like shit

feels like damn

feels like I'm going through hell
In my search for heaven

What is this world we live in?
where you're taught that beauty is skin
Makes you dazed and confused
sets you up to lose
but man, I'm trying to win
So many mistakes I've made
so many times
so many tears
Trying to learn to live
with these regrets of mine

Still it makes me feel like shit
feels like damn
feels like I'm burning inside
Oh it makes me feel like shit
feels like damn
feels like I'm going through hell
In my search for heaven

$\mathfrak{A}$t the beginning of my career, there was one particular incident that really turned my head around. It made me realize that people in this business can constantly put you in an uncomfortable and vulnerable position. I learned this the hard way. By the time I found the courage to voice my feelings, a magazine was already on the newsstands, on *every* corner, with a photograph that embarrassed me, and I had to live with it. There was nothing I could do about it. It was devastating to me because it presented me in a light that I really didn't want to stand in and worse, I hadn't felt comfortable with the photo shoot all along. I just didn't know how to say no to them because I was inexperienced. So I doubted myself, but in my gut I knew the whole time that it wasn't right.

$\mathfrak{l}$ong after, in my mind, I tried to find reasons to justify it, but the only justification I could come up with was that this was something that showed me how strong I would have to be to stand up for what I believe to be true, no matter what some fool thinks. That fool doesn't have to sleep with my conscience every night.

Since it was hard for me to sleep at the time, I sat at my piano and wrote "In My Search for Heaven" to express the thoughts that burned through me.

mr. jealousy

I see the way
You've been reacting
I see the face
That you've been masking
Oh no! It can't be you
I thought you were a friend
But Mr. Jealousy has come to get you, baby

And he's got you green with envy
Known you since I entered this world
But still you're green with envy
Making you a silly girl
Silly girl

You're giving me the blame
To avoid your own

You're slandering my name
For a sympathy vote
Oh no!
I thought you were a friend
But Mr. Jealousy has come to get you, baby

And he's got you
Green with envy
And oh how that just makes my fists curl
Mr. Jealousy is envy
Making you a silly girl
Silly girl

Now don't you try
To apologize
Cause I see you
For who and what you really are
And now I understand
About a fair-weather friend
And it wouldn't be wrong
If
I called you a b*tch
Cause Mr. Jealousy already gotcha, baby

•   •   •

And now you're green with envy
And oh how that just makes my fists curl
Cause now you're green with envy
Making you a silly girl
Silly girl

angel

Sometimes I feel
like I don't belong anywhere
And it's gonna take so long
for me to get somewhere
Sometimes I feel so heavy-hearted
and I can't explain
cause I'm so guarded

But that's a lonely road to travel
and a heavy load to bear
and it's a long, long way to heaven
but I gotta get there

Can you send me an angel?
Please send me an angel
to guide me

•   •   •

Sometimes I feel
like a door with no key
and all the answers are locked away in me
and they're so hard to find
especially when I feel lost and so blind

But that's a lonely road to travel
and a heavy load to bear
and it's a long, long way to heaven
but I gotta get there

Can you send an angel?
Please send an angel
to guide me

Cause I don't wanna feel
like a dove with no wings
and I don't wanna know
what a heart of stone sings

Cause that's a lonely road to travel
and a heavy load to bear

and it's a long, long way to heaven
but I gotta get there

Can you send me an angel?
Please send me an angel
to guide me . . .

no room for religion

No room for religion

No room for morals

Creating false celebrities

To be the spokesperson for their beliefs and products

Don't anyone else see it?

Sadness festers

Intuition nonexistent

Democracy is just a trick for capitalism to win

Get everyone involved

Not to acquire peace

But to get a piece

A piece of everything

Of every country and every government

Casualties only a sacrifice for the greater cause

Of greater power

Making everyone believe all they see

Is all they want

Is all there is

All they want

Is all they see

The average American

Everyone just lusting

After money and power

After sex

After shocking moments

Proud to be a ho

Fame is all there is

To keep us closed

A plan

Only to control

And we fall for it

And for what?

Meanwhile the boys are out there

Consolidating the world

While we're here in oblivion

Working hard to party the money away

To get drunk to forget

What we don't even know

Cause we don't even want to know

There's no room for religion
Only moldable minds

Uninterested in looking beyond
These four walls of a country
Boxing us in
Losing everything
In spite of ourselves
Including ourselves
Souls have a sickness
Called control
But we don't own anything
We only beg and borrow
From the bank
that division of the government
Set up to make more off of our
Simpleminded, uneducated, no-one-told-us-cause-
no-one-ever-knew-themselves ignorance
We get ahead to fall behind
Time and time again
Blindfolded by the American dream
The average American

Meanwhile the boys are out
Following the man

They only just met
But will never trust
To provide justice
That makes no sense
There's no room for religion out there
Slowly eating away at the core
With nothing to believe in

And back at home
We are the same average Americans
With nothing to believe in
But the picture-perfect painting on grandma's wall
That will never be
Cause there's no room for religion in democracy

such a strong word

I HATE EVERY SINGLE FACE I SEE
EVERYONE SITTING NEXT TO ME
EVERY FACE STARING BACK AT ME
I HATE MY EYES FOR BEING SO HEAVY

I HATE THE WAY THEY PRETEND
UNTIL THEY THINK THEY'VE GOTTEN IN
AND THEN ALL THE PRETENDING ENDS
AND COMFORT, LAZINESS AND LACK OF
   FORESIGHT BEGINS

I HATE THE WAY THEY LOOK
ACTING IMPORTANT
I HATE THE WAY THEY KNOW NOTHING
AT ALL
AND ACT LIKE THEY KNOW IT ALL

I HATE THE WAY THAT I DESPISE
THE LOOK IN THEIR EYES

I HATE HOW MY HEART CRIES
AND I HAVE NO ONE TO TELL

I HATE BEING LIKE A MACHINE
I HATE FEELING ALL MEAN
I HATE FEELING DIRTY
BUT I CAN'T COME CLEAN

I HATE THEM STANDING NEXT TO ME
SHADOWING MY EVERY MOVE

I HATE THE WAY THEIR VOICES SOUND
I HATE SEEING THE SAME FACES
I HATE THE WAY THEY TRAIL ME TO
    EVERY PLACE
I HATE THEM TAKING UP SPACE

I HATE CARING SO MUCH
WHEN NO ONE SEEMS TO CARE
I HATE SEEING DOLLAR SIGNS
EVERYWHERE
I HATE THAT I HAVE NO MORE PATIENCE
    TO SPARE
I HATE THAT SHIT AIN'T FAIR

•   •   •

I HATE ALL THESE SOUNDS IN MY HEAD
I DON'T WANNA DIE
I HATE FEELING DEAD
THIS FEELING OF DREAD
I DREAD THE FEELING
I HATE ALL THE THINGS UNSAID
I HATE JUST DEALING

I'M EXHAUSTED
BUT I CAN'T SLEEP
I HATE FEELING THIS HATE SO DEEP

I JUST WANNA SMILE
BUT I HATE BEING FAKE
FEELING LIKE I'M ABOUT TO BREAK
I HATE PEOPLE THAT ONLY SEE ME AS CAKE
TRY TO CAKE UP ON ME, NOW THAT'S A
    MISTAKE
THEY'RE ALL SNAKES
IN ONE WAY OR ANOTHER

everywhere
is nowhere

I've made my home in many places
From New York streets and subway seats
to London's cold and foggy sleets
From hotel rooms in the biggest suites
to motels sick with dirty sheets
In smoky clubs, that barely fit 104
to the largest stage of screaming more!
I've slept quite hard on buses and trains
with daily trips on wide-winged planes
and some days I've often felt very strange
cause something's missing
Got comfortable in the smallest car
with a noisy engine not destined to go far
Found myself lost in some nowhere bar
feeling the scar
of something missing
I've walked the *rues* of Paris

Champs-Elysées and historic places
past all kinds of lonely faces
including my own
cause something's gone
Made it to the mystery of Madrid
the magic of Barcelona
Just a little kitty in a big city
with needles, like threats, layin' in the street
where girls in little no matter the weather
walk the same sad beat
and bright lights and big dreams dance flirtatiously
Made my way to Italy
villages of Lucca
and the little, easy-going city of Palermo
with big hills and midnight seas
I've had my breath stolen from me on the mountains
    of the Alps
looking out at the permanent painted picture of
    perfection in God's land
Understand
I've even touched the golden-red magenta sands of
    the Middle East
while the sun vanished over dunes that looked
    miles high
But no matter where I've slept

No matter where I've gone
in every dark corner I see
our passion rising in front of me
like hot subway steam
hissing with fury
In every dark night I see a knight
and in every bright moon
I see what we have yet to discover
In every sunrise and orange sky
I hear your voice whispering in my ear
In the deep sands I feel your heat
beneath my feet is your heartbeat
In every ocean I feel you sweet with sweat making
     me wet
On every mountaintop I feel your calm, your breeze,
     your breath
In every café you feed me with dreams
cause I can't wait to taste you
can't wait for you to fill me with all that I've been
     missing

And this must be what all those poets are talking
     about
cause everywhere is nowhere if you're not
     somewhere near . . .

lady malasuérte

Everyone should wish to be
as strong as Lady Malasuérte
Both a warrior and an angel
both a peasant and a queen
A woman who loved no harder
than any one of us
but was punished far worse
than by just the pain of a lost or stolen love
by just the pain of a broken heart
Her story is your story
our story is hers

Everyone should wish to be
as forgiving as Lady Malasuérte
Both a warrior and an angel
both a woman and a child
Believing in truth

but riddled with lies
that leave one far more pained
than that of bullets
Her story is your story
our story is hers

Everyone should wish to have
faith as strong as that of Lady Malasuérte
Both haunted and blessed
trapped between hell and heaven
the worst purgatory
Tested every day for her belief in God
in good
and every day fighting to hold on
to sanity
to truth
to life
Though life has drastically changed
to an underworld of metal
and no escape
a world of hate
and little sunshine
a world where even those with whom you sleep
try to make you break

your heart cry
your eyes blank

And while Lady Malasuérte may be no saint
she sure as hell deserves not *this*!
And neither do you
for her story is yours
and our story is hers
and we all make mistakes.

ady Malasuérte" is about a woman who was convicted, unfairly, for something that she did not do. Her story is our story and our story is hers because she represents anyone caught up in a system much more powerful than we are. A system that only serves a green master. She was sentenced to serve over three hundred years in prison and every time I think about it, I think about how close I could be to some unknown, life-altering situation. I know I have been close many times. This reminds me to have faith, strength, and belief even in the most dire of circumstances.

stolen moments

So far apart

But not in the mind

It never mattered there was time between us

Somehow it was like

A message

And that's how I knew it was right

The stars of the night

Told me

Twinkling so brightly.

Had to hide

So discreetly

But couldn't stop

The shining

In the eyes

When I think of you

In the mouth

When I speak of you

In the hands
When I touch you.

Remembering the days
When our love began
Thinking of a million ways
To escape and be with you
But reality wasn't just you and I
It was long, drawn-out days and lonely nights

Dreaming about you
I keep dreaming about you
And I'm dreaming about when you would say

Let me take you to another place
where nothing ever seems to matter
it's just you and me
we can take flight like a thief in the night
stolen moments with you

Destiny
Didn't have such a simple plan
I was just a girl
And you were a man
How could age define

Something so divine?
Can this even be real or just exist in my mind?

Dreaming about you
I keep dreaming about you
And I'm dreaming about when you would say

Let me take you to another place
where nothing ever seems to matter
it's just you and me
we can take flight like a thief in the night
stolen moments with you

4 letter word

It's a cold, cold summer's winter
It's a day as dark as night
It's the hottest heat in December
It's the blindest part of sight

It's what you hear in your head when you're all alone
It's the honest part in you
It's the smallest thing makes you feel so large
And it leaves you all confused

It makes a soldier of a coward
Makes the bravest man cry
It makes death feel like heaven
And makes you scared to die

It's all for just a 4 letter word
A simple 4 letter word

•   •   •

It's the coldest part of a heart so warm
It's a dark as bright as day
It's alive in the ones that feel good is gone
And it carries you away

It's what you hear in your heart when you're all
    alone
It's the evil part in you
It's the smallest thing makes you feel so tall
But it's got you all confused

It makes a soldier look like a coward
Makes the weakest think they're brave
With it no one enters heaven
Sends you to an early grave

It's all for just a 4 letter word
A simple 4 letter word

when gone
is the glory

When gone is the glory
When gone is the fame
When gone is the name
And you're left with yourself

You look in the mirror
To search your face
To remember who you are
Who you ever were

When gone is the glory
When gone is the shine
Is gone the whole
Of your fortune and pride?

You look all around
In search of a friend

That no longer stands
Until the "bitter end"

When gone is the glory
When gone is the sun
When gone is the game
Then what have you won?

Heartache and pain
Of what could have been
Only you know the truth
Of what lies within

When gone is the praise
When gone is the fun
Is gone the worth
Of what you have become?

When I'm left alone
At the end of this story
How does it feel
When gone is the glory

from
songs in A minor

girlfriend

Maybe silly for me to feel
This way about you and her
Cause I know she's been
Such a good friend
I know she has helped you through

Talkin' late on the phone
Every night you've been calling
Private moments alone
Could your heart soon be falling
And I know she's a friend
But I can't shake the feeling
That I could be losing your heart

I think I'm jealous of your girlfriend
Although she's just a girl that is your friend
I think I'm jealous of your girlfriend

Cause she shares a special part of you
Oh, oh

You said that she's
One who helped you see
How deep you're in love with me
And intentions were not
To get in between
But I see possibilities

And you say that you feel
I'm the best thing in your life
And I know it's real
I see it in your eyes
There's no reason for me
To even feel this way
I know you just enjoy her company

I think I'm jealous of your girlfriend
Although she's just a girl that is your friend
I think I'm jealous of your girlfriend
Cause she shares a special part of you
Oh, oh

fallin'

I keep on fallin'
In and out of love with you
Sometimes I love you
Sometimes you make me blue
Sometimes I feel good
At times I feel used
Loving you, darling
Makes me so confused

I keep on fallin'
In and out of love with you
I never loved someone
The way that I'm lovin' you

Oh, oh I
Never felt this way
How do you give me so much pleasure

And cause me so much pain
And just when I think
I've taken more than would a fool
I start fallin' back in love with you

I keep on fallin'
In and out of love with you
I never loved someone
The way that I'm lovin' you

I'm fallin'
I'm fallin'
I'm fallin'
Fallin'

I keep on fallin'
In and out of love with you
I never loved someone
The way that I'm lovin' you

troubles

Feels like the world is closing in on me
Feels like my dreams will never come to be
I keep on slipping deeper into myself
And I'm scared
So scared

If you're troubled
You just gotta let it go
If you're worried, baby
You just gotta let it go
All your hustles ain't for nothing
You just gotta take it slow
When you need me, baby
All you do is let me know

Why do I feel
That my mind is constantly tryin'

To pull me down
I can't seem to get away
Continuous mistakes I know I made before
How long will I feel so out of place?

If you're troubled
You just gotta let it go
If you're worried, baby
You just gotta let it go
All your hustles ain't for nothing
You just gotta take it slow
When you need me, baby
All you do is let me know

rock with you

There's no escape
From the spell you have placed
Deep in my heart and mind
Foolish am I
If I were to try
To ever leave you behind

I wanna rock with you
Don't matter what we do
With you and only you
I wanna rock with you

I'll stay and walk this life with you
No matter what we may go through
Dead broke no job no house no ride
I'm gonna stay right by your side

. . .

I wanna rock with you
Don't matter what we do
With you and only you
I wanna rock with you

You question where you're headed to
But love, don't be afraid
To trust, believe in us

I wanna rock with you
Don't matter what we do
With you and only you
I wanna rock with you

a woman's worth

You could buy me diamonds
You could buy me pearls
Take me on a cruise around the world
Baby, you know I'm worth it

Dinner lit by candles
Run my bubble bath
Make love tenderly to last and last
Baby, you know I'm worth it

Wanna please, wanna keep, wanna treat your
   woman right?
Not just dough, better show, that you know she's
   worth your time
You will lose, if you choose, to refuse to put her first
She will and she can find a man who knows her worth!

• • •

Cause a real man knows a real woman when he
    sees her
And a real woman knows a real man
Ain't 'fraid to please her
And a real woman knows a real man always
    comes first
And a real man just can't deny
A woman's worth

If you can treat me fairly
I'll give you all my goods
Treat you like a real woman should
Baby, I know you're worth it

If you never play with me
Promise not to bluff
I'll hold you down when shit gets rough
Cause baby, I know you're worth it

She walks the mile, makes you smile, all the while
    being true
Don't take for granted the passions that she has
    for you
You will lose, if you choose, to refuse to put her first

She will and she can find a man who knows
  her worth!

Oh!

Cause a real man knows a real woman when he
  sees her
And a real woman knows a real man
Ain't 'fraid to please her
And a real woman knows a real man always
  comes first
And a real man just can't deny
A woman's worth

No need to read between the lines
Spelled out for you
Just hear this song
Cause you can't go wrong
When you value a woman's worth

Cause a real man knows a real woman when he
  sees her
And a real woman knows a real man
Ain't 'fraid to please her

And a real woman knows a real man always
    comes first
And a real man just can't deny
A woman's worth

jane doe

Let's talk about the situation
'Bout how you came with information
That's negative in every which way
Just dissin' my man and our relations

You say he's cheatin', want me to leave him
I changed my mind I think I'll keep him
Listenin' to you will leave me lonely
That's not what I'm tryin' to be

Cause I'd be crazy to let my man go
And let some other Jane Doe
Come and try to steal him
Oh no, oh no!

Just crazy to let my man go
And let some other Jane Doe
Come and try to steal him
Oh no, oh no!

Caughtcha tryin' to check my man out
How about you s'plain what that's all about
Think you slick like I wouldn't know
But I got something for you though

Mess around end up in choke hold
Girl, I think it's time for you to go
Away from my man and me
That's the way it's gonna be

Cause I'd be crazy to let my man go
And let some other Jane Doe
Come and try to steal him
Oh no, oh no!
Just crazy to let my man go
And let some other Jane Doe
Come and try to steal him
Oh no, oh no!

•   •   •

I love my man

He loves me more

May not be the perfect man but

I don't plan to let him go for

Jane Doe

goodbye

How do you love someone
That hurts you so bad
With intentions good
Was all he ever had
But how do I let go when I
Loved him for so long I've
Given him all that I could?
Maybe love is a hopeless crime
Given up what seems your lifetime
What went wrong with something once so good?

How do you find the words to say
To say goodbye
When your heart don't have the heart to say
To say goodbye

•   •   •

I know now I was naïve

Never knew where this would lead

And I'm not tryin' to take away

From the good man that he is

But how do I let go when I

Loved him for so long I've

Given him all that I could

Was it something wrong that we did

Or cause others infiltrated

What went wrong with something once so good?

How do you find the words to say

To say goodbye

When your heart don't have the heart to say

To say goodbye

Is this the end?

Are you sure?

How should you know when you've

Never been here before?

It's so hard

To just let go

When this is the one and only
Love I've ever known

How do you find the words to say
To say goodbye
When your heart don't have the heart to say
To say goodbye

the life

Every day I realize

That this may be the last day of my life

Walking down the street I find

I'm coming closer and closer to losing my mind

Cause when it rains it pours

Isn't life worth more?

I don't even know what I'm hustling for

You gotta do what you gotta do

Just to make it through

All the hard times that's gonna face you

This is the life

Striving to survive

Living will always be a struggle

Looking for someone true to love you

Looking back I see all the horror

This madness makes me wanna holler

I watch slowly,

Internally I'm dying

Pillowcase is wet from all my crying

And there is nothing more

To be here for

Take me away

I can't take this life no more

This is the life

Striving to survive

mister man

Something about the way you smiled at me just drove
   me wild
Wish I could know if you're alone don't want to
   cramp your style
But I cannot deny
The feel that I feel
When I look into your eyes
Feel my heart beating fast for
A challenge may arise

I wanna know if you feel the way I do
I do
I wanna know if there's a chance for me and you
And you
If there's no way meet at the bar and say you can't
You can't
Cause I don't wanna be
I don't wanna be

I don't wanna be
Unfair to Mister Man

I like the way you've given me attention through the
    night
Maybe I've had too much Rémy my man's right by my
    side
Every time I catch you watching me
I feel something down my spine
I'll play the game it's just for fun and only for tonight

I wanna know what makes you feel the way you do
You do
I think you're hoping there's a chance for me and you
And you
Should I meet you at the bar and say we can't
We can't
Cause I don't wanna be
I don't wanna be
I don't wanna be unfair to Mister Man

I know all you wanna know is answers
Cause you can give me what I need
We both know that we're attracted
Should we let our desires lead?

butterflyz

Lately when I look into your eyes I realize
You're the only one I need in my life
Baby, I just don't know how to describe
How lovely you make me feel inside

You give me butterflyz
Got me flyin' so high in the sky
I can't control
The butterflyz

It seemed like a likely thing
From the start you told me
I would be your queen
But never had I imagined such a feeling
Joy is what you bring
I wanna give you everything

*   *   *

You give me butterflyz
Got me flyin' so high in the sky
I can't control
The butterflyz

You and I are destiny
I know now
You were made for me

You give me butterflyz
Got me flyin' so high in the sky
I can't control
The butterflyz

why do i feel so sad?

Friends we've been for so long

Now true colors are showing

Makes me wanna cry

Oh yes it does

Cause I have to say goodbye

By now I should know

That in time things must change

So it shouldn't be so bad

So why do I feel so sad?

How can I adjust to the way that things are going?

It's killing me slowly

Oh I just want it to be how it used to be

I wish I could stay

But in time things must change

So it shouldn't be so bad
So why do I feel so sad?

You cannot hide the way you feel inside
I realize
Your actions speak much louder than words

By now I should know
That in time things must change
So it shouldn't be so bad
So why do I feel so sad?

caged bird

Right now I feel like a bird
Caged without a key
Everyone comes to stare at me
With so much joy and revelry

They don't know how I feel inside
Through my smile I cry
They don't know what they're doing to me
Keeping me from flyin'

That's why I say that
I know why the caged bird sings
Her only joy comes from song
If she's so rare and beautiful to others
Why not set her free?

• • •

So she can fly, fly, fly

Spreading her wings and her song

Let her fly, fly, fly

For the whole world to see

She's like a caged bird

Fly, fly oh

Just let her fly

Just let her fly

Spread the wings, spread the beauty . . .

lovin' you

If I gave you forever
would you take care of me?
or would you take me for granted
and run away?

Those wonderful things that you do
they got me feeling in love with you
in love with you

Lovin' you is easy
it comes so naturally
lovin' you is easy
it comes so naturally

I will give you laughter
and oh so much more than that
oh, yes I will

anything you're after
I'll climb the highest mountain
to bring it back
you better believe

Those wonderful things that you do
they got me feeling in love with you
in love with you

Lovin' you is easy
it comes so naturally
lovin' you is easy
it comes so naturally   .

I will stay by your side
whether I'm wrong, whether I'm right
oh it's incredible
with you I intend to spend the rest of my life

from the diary
of alicia keys

karma

Weren't you the one that said that you don't want me
   anymore
And how you need your space and give the keys back
   to your door
And how I cried and tried and tried to make you stay
   with me
And still you said the love was gone and that I had
   to leave

Now you're talking 'bout a family
Now you're saying I complete your dreams
Now you're sayin' I'm your everything
You're confusing me
What you saying to me, don't play with me, don't play
   with me
Cause . . .

.   .   .

135

What goes around comes around

What goes up must come down

Now who's cryin', desirin' to come back to me?

What goes around comes around

What goes up must come down

Now who's cryin', desirin', to come back

I remember when I was sittin' home alone

Waitin' for you till three o'clock in the morn

And when you came home you'd always have some
sorry excuse

Half explaining to me like I'm just some kind of
a fool

I sacrificed the things I wanted just to do things
for you

But when it's time to do for me

You never come through

Now you wanna be up under me

Now you have so much to say to me

Now you wanna make time for me

Whatcha doin' to me, you're confusin' me

Don't play with me don't play with me cause

What goes around comes around

What goes up must come down

Now who's cryin', desirin' to come back to me?
What goes around comes around
What goes up must come down
Now who's cryin', desirin', to come back

I remember when I was sittin' home alone
Waitin' for you till three o'clock in the morn
Night after night knowing something's goin' on
Wasn't long before I be gone
Lord knows it wasn't easy, believe me
Never thought you'd be the one that would deceive me
And never do what you're supposed to do
No need to approach me fool, cause I'm over you

What goes around comes around
What goes up must come down
Now who's cryin', desirin' to come back to me?
What goes around comes around
What goes up must come down
Now who's cryin', desirin', to come back

Gotta stop trying to come back to me
It's called karma, baby, and it goes around

heartburn

Uh. Yeah. Come on. Timbo! A. Keys,
Let's go!

Let me tell you something
Tell you how I feel
When he comes around
I get to feelin' ill
It's an aching feelin' inside my chest
It's like I'm goin' into cardiac arrest

Adrenaline rushing in my body
All my power I just can't fight it
No matter how I keep on tryin'
I can't deny I got this . . . heartburn
Burnin' in my soul
Call the fire department
It's out of control

· · ·

Got me trippin', slippin', gettin' beside myself
I tried some medication but don't nothin' help
So I said, "Docta, Docta, tell me will I die?"
And he said, *"Count to five, Alicia"*
And I'm gonna be all right, let's go! 1, 2, 3, 4 . . .

Adrenaline rushing in my body
All my power I just can't fight it
No matter how I keep on tryin'
I can't deny I got this . . . heartburn
Burnin' in my soul
Call the fire department
It's out of control

Tastes so good I can't resist
Getting harder to digest
Can't take no more
Gotta shake it off, and break it down
And take it to the ground with me now
Everybody say *Oooohhhh . . .*

•   •   •

Don't you know I got this . . . heartburn
Burnin' in my soul
Call the fire department
It's out of control

What you tryin' to do?

you don't know
my name

Baby, baby, baby
From the day I saw you
I really, really wanted to catch your eye
There's something special 'bout you
I must really like you
Cause not a lotta guys are worth my time
Ooo baby, baby, baby
It's gettin' kind of crazy
Cause you are takin' over my mind

And it feels like ooooo
But you don't know my name
And I swear it feels like ooooo ooooo ooooo ooooo
You don't know my name
(round and round and round we go, will you
ever know?)

           •   •   ■

Oh baby, baby, baby
I see us on our first date
You're doin' everything that makes me smile
And when we had our first kiss
It happened on a Thursday
Ooooo it set my soul on fire
Ooo baby, baby, baby
I can't wait for the first time
My imagination's runnin' wild

It feels like ooooo
You don't know my name
And I swear it, baby, it feels like ooooo ooooo
    ooooo ooooo
You don't know my name
(round and round and round we go, will you
    ever know?)

"I'm sayin', he don't even know what he's doin' to me
Got me feelin' all crazy inside
I'm feelin' like"
Oh!

I'm doin' more than I've ever done for anyone's
    attention

Take notice of what's in front of you

Cause did I mention you're 'bout to miss a good thing

And you'll never know how good it feels to have all of
   my affection

And you'll never get a chance to experience my lovin'

Cause my lovin' feels like ooooo

You don't know my name

(round and round and round we go, will you
   ever know?)

And I swear it feels like ooooo ooooo ooooo ooooo

You don't know my name

(round and round and round we go, will you
   ever know?)

Will you ever know it?

No, no, no, no, no

Will you ever know it?

"Well, I'm gonna have to just go ahead and call this boy.

Hello? Can I speak to—to Michael?

Oh hey, how you doin'?

Uh, I feel kinda silly doin' this,

*But um, this is the waitress from the coffeehouse on
   Thirty-ninth and Lenox*

You know, the one with the braids?

Yeah, well, I see you on Wednesdays all the time
You come in every Wednesday on your lunch break,
    I think
And you always order the special, with the hot chocolate
And my manager be tripping and stuff
Talking 'bout we gotta use water
But I always use some milk and cream for you
Cause I think you're kinda sweet.
Anyway you always got on some fly blue suit
'n' your cufflinks are shining all bright
So, whatchu do? Oh, word? Yeah, that's interesting
Look man, I mean, I don't wanna waste your time but
I know girls don't usually do this,
But I was wondering if maybe we could get together
Outside the restaurant one day
Cause I do look a lot different outside my work clothes
I mean, we could just go across the street to the park
    right here
Wait, hold up, my cell phone's breakin' up, hold up
Can you hear me now? Yeah
So, what day did you say?
Oh yeah, Thursday's perfect, man . . ."

if i ain't got you

Some people live for the fortune

Some people live just for the fame

Some people live for the power, yeah

Some people live just to play the game

Some people think that the physical things

Define what's within

And I've been there before

But that life's a bore

So full of the superficial

Some people want it all

But I don't want nothing at all

If it ain't you, baby

If I ain't got you, baby

Some people want diamond rings

Some just want everything

But everything means nothing
If I ain't got you, yeah

Some people search for a fountain
That promises forever young
Some people need three dozen roses
And that's the only way to prove you love them
Hand me the world on a silver platter
And what good would it be
With no one to share
with no one who truly cares for me

Some people want it all
But I don't want nothing at all
If it ain't you, baby
If I ain't got you, baby
Some people want diamond rings
Some just want everything
But everything means nothing
If I ain't got you

If I ain't got you with me, baby
Nothing in this whole wide world don't mean
    a thing
If I ain't got you with me, baby

diary

Lay your head on my pillow
Here you can be yourself
No one has to know what you are feeling
No one but me and you

I won't tell your secrets
Your secrets are safe with me
I will keep your secrets
Just think of me as the pages in your diary

I feel such a connection
Even when you're far away
Oooh, baby, if there is anything that you fear
Call and I'll be here

I won't tell your secrets
Your secrets are safe with me

I will keep your secrets
Just think of me as the pages in your diary

Only we know what is talked about, Baby boy
Don't know how you could be driving me so crazy
Baby, when you're in town
Why don't you come around
I'll be the loyalty you need
You can trust me

I won't tell your secrets
Your secrets are safe with me
I will keep your secrets
Just think of me as the pages in your diary

dragon days

Like a damsel in distress
I'm stressing you
My castle became a dungeon cause I'm longing
    for you (longing for you, babe)
I'm feeling strong for ya
You're my knight in shining armor
See your face in the silver moon
Hung low over the lagoon
And it feels like

Dragon days and the fire's hot
Like a desert needs water
I need you a lot
Dragon days
I need to be saved
I'm missin' you
And the days drag on and on

•   •   •

I'm desperate for ya, baby

Do you know what that means?

It means I feel like an addict must feel

When he fiends

In an act of desperation I get lost in ma dreams

Cause like a lady in waiting

I'm waiting for ya

Like a prisoner tied over alligator waters

Waiting for my prince of paradise to come and take
    me away

From these

Tick tock, tick tock

Dragon days and the fire's hot

Like a desert needs water

I need you a lot

Dragon days

I need to be saved

I'm missin' you

And the days drag on and on

wake up

You used to be my closest ally
In this cold, cold world of deception and lies
We would defend and protect one another
Now I can't tell if we're enemies or lovers

So who's gonna rescue us from ourselves?

When we gonna wake up, baby?
When it's time for lovin'
When we gonna wake up
Before it's too late?

Oh, baby, where did we go wrong, baby?
Did this cold, cold world turn us into stone?
Now all I battle is your ego and your pride
It's ticking like a time bomb, ready to ignite
Hurtin' me to fight

      •   •   •

Who's gonna rescue us from ourselves?

When we gonna wake up, baby?
When it's time for lovin'
When we gonna wake up
Before it's too late?

When the smoke clears
What will be left for us but tears and pain
Why must we argue over the same things
Just to make up and go back again
It's never too late
But it's been too long
Can't get it right
When no one thinks they're wrong
Gotta get out of bed
And take a look at what's going on

When we gonna wake up, baby?
When it's time for lovin'
When we gonna wake up
Before it's too late?

so simple

What it is ain't what it was
What should it be?
When it comes to you and . . .
How it seems ain't how it is
There's been a change
When it comes to me and . . .

Oh, baby, you
Oh, baby, me
Oh maybe we can try another day
Another way
All in my mind
I'm wondering why we cannot find
What was left at the beginning
If I could

●　　●　　●

Meet you again,

Miss you again,

Kiss you again

It would be so simple

Cause I would love you again

Hold you again

Need you again

It would be, it would be

Could it be, could it be so simple

Now it's hardly simple,

It's just simply hard

When it comes to you and

I find myself not being myself

Just to avoid all this confrontation with

Oh, baby, you

Oh, baby, me

Oh maybe we can put this armor down

And settle down

Oh it's off track

That is a fact

Can we get it back?

Get it back to the beginning

. . .

If I could meet you again,

Miss you again,

Kiss you again

It would be so simple

Cause I would love you again

Hold you again

Need you again

It would be, it would be

Could it be, could it be so simple

Don't you know that it would be

So simple

when you really love someone

I'm a woman and Lord knows it's hard
I need a real man to give me what I need
Sweet attention, love and tenderness
When it's real it's unconditional, I'm telling y'all

Cause a man just ain't a man,
if he ain't man enough
to love you when you're right,
love you when you're wrong
love you when you're weak,
love you when you're strong
take you higher
when the world got you feelin' low

He's giving you his last, cause he's thinking of
    you first
Giving comfort when he's thinking that you're hurt

That's what's done when you really love someone
I'm telling y'all, I'm telling y'all

Cause you're a real man and Lord knows it's hard
Sometimes you just need a woman's touch
Sweet affection, love and support
When it's real, it's unconditional, I'm telling y'all

Oh cause a woman ain't a woman if she ain't
    woman enough
to love you when you're right
love you when you're wrong
love you when you're weak,
love you when you're strong
take you higher
when the world got you feelin' low

She's giving you her best, even when you're at
    your worst
Giving comfort, when she's thinking that you're hurt
That's what's done, when you really love someone
I'm telling y'all

Sometimes you gonna argue
Sometimes you gonna fight

Sometimes it's gonna feel like it will never be right
But something so strong, keeps you holdin' on
It don't make sense, but it makes a good song

Cause a man just ain't a man,
if he ain't man enough
to love you when you're right,
love you when you're wrong
love you when you're weak,
love you when you're strong
take you higher
when the world's got you feelin' low

He's giving you his last, cause he's thinking of
    you first
Giving comfort when he's thinking that you're hurt
That's what's done when you really love someone
I'm telling y'all, I'm telling y'all, I'm telling y'all

That a woman ain't a woman if she ain't
    woman enough
To love you when you're right,
love you when you're wrong
love you when you're weak,
love you when you're strong

take you higher
when the world's got you feelin' low

She's giving you her best, even when you're at
   worst
Giving comfort, when she's thinking that you're hurt
That's what's done, when you really love someone
I'm telling y'all
I'm telling y'all

slow down

Ooooo, baby
There's something that I gotta tell ya
I think that you should know what's on my mind
Ooo, baby I'm feelin' our situation
is getting stronger how we want it
But I gotta take my time

There's so much about you that I want to explore
Physical attraction, we just can't ignore it,
But before we go too far across the line
Gotta really make sure that I'm sure

Slow down, baby, let's take our time
Slow down, baby, if you don't mind
Slow down, baby, before we make this move
Slow down, baby,
I think it's really too soon

•   •   •

Ooo, baby, it's like I've known you forever
My medulla oblongata is electrified
Ooo, baby, whenever we're alone together
'Bout to explode and it feels so right
But I gotta take my time

There's so much about you that I want to explore
Physical attraction, we just can't ignore it,
But before we go too far across the line
Gotta really make sure that I'm sure

Slow down, baby, let's take our time
Slow down, baby, if you don't mind
Slow down, baby, before we make this move
Slow down, baby,
I think it's really too soon

See, I know what is best, cause I've been there before
Gave myself to someone for all the wrong reasons
But this time around, I don't want to do that again
I just want to make this the way that I've dreamed of

samsonite man

He's a man so full of style and grace
Any woman'd be impressed
Takes a smile and paints it on your face
Makes you feel like you've been blessed
Promises things so special
It seems to come right from a song
But soon as you begin to feel secure
You turn around and he is gone

Packin' his bags
Gotta go, gotta go
Packin' his bags
Gotta go
He's a Samsonite man

Maybe he is just a rolling stone
Wandering from here to there

Searching for a place to call his own
You wonder if he even cares
So many years of heartache and pain
Is all you seem to know him for
Is it you or is it he to blame
Whenever he walks out your door

Packin' his bags
Gotta go, gotta go
Packin' his bags
Gotta go
He's a Samsonite man

Should the wind blow you in my direction
And you come through to rendezvous
Forget about your good intentions,
They leave me lonely and confused
Mr. Samsonite
Pack a bag, that is my suggestion
From here on out, you will be leaving
At *my* discretion!

•   •   •

Packin' his bags

Gotta go, gotta go

Packin' his bags

Gotta go

He's a Samsonite man

nobody, not really

Who really cares?
Who really cares?
When I talk?
What I feel?
What I say?
Nobody, not really

Who wants to take
The time to understand?
I would like
Someone to heal me with some empathy
But I can't find
Nobody, not really

Maybe I'm invisible to the world
Does anyone in the world even think of me
As more than just a hopeless cause

Maybe the world is not my block
My stoop
My life, my dreams
My anything

So, who wants to help?
Momma, but she's so tired
Papa, but you're not here
I'm alone in a big empty space with
Nobody, not really

acknowledgments

my *best friend, favorite editor, and best kept secret*: Momma, there's just no one like you! You introduced me to this world of reading that I have come to adore. You are the reason I can get lost in a book and that is the reason I have the strength, courage, and love to create my own.

My Nana: I cannot do anything without thanking you. You are the reason for so much of the woman I've become. You wrapped your arms around me at all the right times and pushed me at all the right moments.

Fafa: I know it's you guiding me from above.

Jeff: For always telling me to keep writing and for being my bridge.

Krucial: My most influential and beloved muse.

Jeanine: For all the efficiency and care.

Rose: No words will ever do a sister's love justice. I know you understand what I'm saying. There's no one like you . . .

The special people who are my rocks: Your support gives me strength.

Everyone at Putnam and Berkley: For being a part of the big vision. This feels like the beginning of something grand!

    Step 1
    Complete
    More to come
    Nothing will ever stop
    The drum
    Of my heartbeat

Alicia

credits

from *songs in A minor*

"Girlfriend": (Alicia Keys, Jermaine Dupri, Joshua Thompson, Derrick Harris, Russell Jones) Copyright © 2001 by Lellow Productions, EMI April Music, Inc., So So Def Music, Tallest Tree Music, Nassir Music, Inc., Warner-Tamerlane Publishing Co., Wu Tang Publishing, Inc. All rights for Lellow Productions and So So Def Music administered by EMI April Music, Inc. (ASCAP). All rights for Tallest Tree Music administered by Cherry Lane Music Publishing (ASCAP). All rights for Wu Tang Publishing, Inc. administered by Warner-Tamerlane Publishing Co. (BMI)

"Fallin'": (Alicia Keys) Copyright © 2001 by Lellow Productions and EMI April Music, Inc. All rights administered by EMI April Music, Inc. (ASCAP)

All rights administered by EMI April Music, Inc. (ASCAP)

"Lovin' You": (Alicia Keys) Copyright © 2001 by Lellow Productions and EMI April Music, Inc. All rights administered by EMI April Music, Inc. (ASCAP)

from *the diary of alicia keys*

"Karma": (Kerry Brothers, Jr., Taneisha Smith, Alicia Keys) Copyright © 2003 by Lellow Productions, EMI April Music, Inc., Book of Daniel Music and Taneisha Smith. All rights administered by EMI April Music, Inc. (ASCAP)

"Heartburn": (Alicia Keys, T. Mosley, Walter Milsap III, Candice Nelson, Erika Rose, "Timbaland") Copyright © 2003 by Lellow Productions, KrucialKeys2Life Music, EMI April Music, Inc., Phoenix Rose Music Publishing, Conjunction Music Pub., Bread Winner Entertainment, Virginia Beach Music and WB Music Corp. All rights for Lellow Productions, KrucialKeys2Life Music, Phoenix Rose Music Publishing and Conjunction

"Dragon Days": (Alicia Keys) Copyright © 2003 by Lellow Productions and EMI April Music, Inc. All rights administered by EMI April Music, Inc. (ASCAP)

"Wake Up": (Alicia Keys, Kerry Brothers, Jr.) Copyright © 2003 by Lellow Productions, EMI April Music, Inc. and Book of Daniel Music. All rights administered by EMI April Music, Inc. (ASCAP)

"So Simple": (Alicia Keys, Harold Lilly, Andre Harris, Vidal Davis) Copyright © 2003 by Lellow Productions, EMI April Music, Inc., Uncle Bobby Music, EMI Blackwood Music, Inc., Dirty Dre Music and Double Oh Eight Music. All rights for Lellow Productions administered by EMI April Music, Inc. (ASCAP). All rights for Uncle Bobby Music administered by EMI Blackwood Music, Inc. (BMI). All rights for Dirty Dre Music and Double Oh Eight Music administered by Universal Music Publishing Group (ASCAP)

"When You Really Love Someone": (Alicia Keys, Kerry Brothers, Jr.) Copyright © 2003 by Lellow Productions, EMI April Music, Inc. and Book of Daniel Music. All rights administered by EMI April Music, Inc. (ASCAP)